AUSTRALIA'S MOST
DANGEROUS
SNAKES

—

By Kathy Riley

Australian
GEOGRAPHIC

AUSTRALIA'S MOST DANGEROUS SNAKES

Text Kathy Riley
Editor Averil Moffat
Art Director: Mike Ellott
Picture research Maisie Keep, Jess Teideman
Print production Chris Clear
Education Coordinator Lauren Smith
Managing Director Matthew Stanton
Associate Publisher, Specialist Division Jo Runciman
Editor-in-Chief, Australian Geographic Chrissie Goldrick

First published in 2014 by:

MEDIA GROUP

Bauer Media
54 Park Street, Sydney, NSW 2000
Telephone (02) 9263 9813, Fax (02) 9216 3731
Email editorial@ausgeo.com.au

www.australiangeographic.com.au

Australian Geographic customer service:
1300 555 176 (local call rate within Australia).
From overseas +61 2 8667 5295

National Library of Australia
Cataloguing-in-Publication entry:

Riley, Kathy, author.
Australia's most dangerous snakes / Kathy Riley.

ISBN 9781742455075 (paperback)

Poisonous snakes – Australia – Juvenile literature.
Poisonous snakes – Australia – Identification – Juvenile literature.
Poisonous snakes--Habitat--Australia--Juvenile literature.
Poisonous snakes--Behavior--Australia--Juvenile literature.
Dangerous animals--Australia--Juvenile literature.

597.960994

Printed in China by Leo Paper Products

OTHER TITLES IN THIS SERIES:

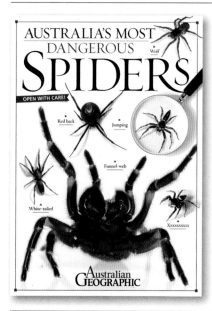

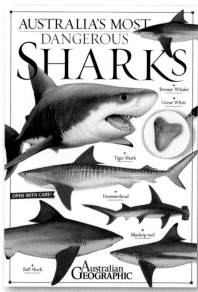

AUSTRALIA'S MOST DANGEROUS SNAKES

CONTENTS

SNAKE PEEK

Snakes are reptiles, which means they are cold-blooded, lay eggs and have scales. All snakes are carnivorous, which means they mostly eat meat. Snakes might appear scary, but take a closer look – they're actually pretty amazing!

FACT BOX — Super scales

The scales on a snake are incredibly useful. They help to protect it, and also stop it from drying out. Scales help the snake to move smoothly, without using too much energy. They may look slimy, but they are actually quite dry. Some snakes are very smooth, while others feel rough.

EFFICIENT EATER

FACT BOX — Eat and breathe

When we have a mouth full of food we can only breathe through our noses. A snake can still breathe through its mouth when it is eating – this is because its windpipe sticks out of the bottom of its mouth. Pretty clever!

Did you know?

Snakes have an organ in their mouth, called a Jacobson's organ. Their tongue picks up chemicals from the air and passes them to this organ, which helps the snake track prey.

PIT

Some snakes have special pits behind their nostrils, which they use to sense temperature changes in the air around them. This helps them to track down the warm bodies of their prey.

EYES

Snakes don't have eyelids; instead, they have a clear scale covering each eye. This protects the eye from damage.

NOSTRIL

A snake only uses its nostrils for breathing, not for smelling. It uses its tongue for smelling.

Nostril

Vertical pupil

Eye

Venom gland

Scales

Pit

Movable maxillary

Venom-conducting tube

Venom canal

Fang

Glottis

Tooth

Tongue sheath

Forked tongue

VENOM GLAND

This is where the venom is produced. Not all snakes have venom. Venom is a kind of poisonous saliva, which travels through the fangs and is injected into prey to kill or stun it.

FANGS

This snake has fangs in the front of its mouth; some snakes have fangs in the back of their mouth. A snake uses its fangs to grasp prey. Venomous snakes inject venom through their fangs.

TONGUE

The flicking, forked tongue picks up tiny **particles** from the air, which tell the snake everything about its surroundings. Snakes are VERY good at using their tongues to 'smell' what is going on around them.

FACT BOX Cold blood

Snakes are **cold-blooded,** which means their body temperature depends on the temperature around them. Snakes need to be warm in order to move or digest food, so they sometimes sun bake in the morning. If it is too hot they find somewhere cool to hide.

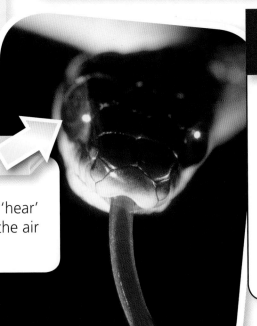

FACT BOX No ears!

Snakes don't have any ears. They 'hear' by picking up on vibrations from the air and the ground.

A Snake's LIFE

All snakes go through the same life cycle. The only big difference is that some snakes lay eggs, while others give birth to live young.

▼ **HATCHING**
The length of time it takes for the eggs to hatch depends on the species and the temperature of the eggs. It can take as long as a couple of months. The baby snake uses a special tooth, called an egg tooth, to help it break out of its shell. It loses this tooth soon after hatching.

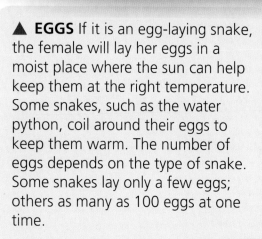

▲ **EGGS** If it is an egg-laying snake, the female will lay her eggs in a moist place where the sun can help keep them at the right temperature. Some snakes, such as the water python, coil around their eggs to keep them warm. The number of eggs depends on the type of snake. Some snakes lay only a few eggs; others as many as 100 eggs at one time.

Did you know?

Baby snakes are left on their own after they are born and are perfect prey for predators. Less than one in 10 newborn snakes survive.

▼ **MATING** Snakes usually mate in spring when the cold weather is over. The male will move over the female, rubbing her body with his chin. Sometimes the male and female get all twisted up together like a piece of liquorice!

Q&A

Q: How long do snakes live?

A: It depends on the species – some snakes will only live a couple of years, while others will live for up to 25 years.

▲ **SHEDDING** As they grow, snakes shed their skin. This is also called moulting. Young snakes moult more often than older snakes because they are growing more quickly. When a snake is just about to moult, the scales over its eyes turn light blue. Once the skin is shed, the snakes' eyes go back to their normal colour. The snake's skin peels off in one piece like a sock. Underneath is a clean, fresh skin that fits perfectly!

FACT BOX   **Winter sleep**

Snakes don't like cold weather because it makes them slow down. In really cold places, snakes **hibernate** through winter. This means they find a safe place and go into a type of deep sleep. This helps them save energy and survive a long time without food. When it gets warmer, they come out of their hiding place and go hunting for food.

RED -BELLIED BLACK SNAKE

Fact File ▼

Found: along the east coast of Australia

Lives: in burrows, hollow logs and beneath rocks in places where there is water

Breeding: gives birth to up to 40 live young at once

Diet: mainly frogs, but also lizards, mammals, birds and fish

SNAKE SCALE — **DANGEROUS**

Length: up to 1.5 metres

True or False?

A red-bellied black snake will eat another red-bellied black snake.

A: True

Did you know?

Red-bellied black snakes will eat canned dog food!

FACT BOX — Hissy fit

Although it is dangerously venomous, the red-bellied black snake is shy and unlikely to bite. Instead, it will put on a scary display, hissing and flattening its neck aggressively.

Skilled swimmers

These snakes are just as happy hunting in water as they are on land. They like to eat fish and tadpoles as well as land-based animals. They can even feed under water.

SWALLOW THIS!

Snakes are mostly very slender and have quite small heads, and yet they are capable of eating quite large animals. How do they do it?

FACT BOX

Meaty menu

▲ All snakes are carnivorous, which means they only eat other animals. This includes smaller animals such as insects, mice, lizards, frogs, other snakes, snails and eggs – as well as much bigger animals, such as birds, cats and chickens. Although it only has a very narrow body, a snake can fit a lot of differently sized animals into it!

Unbelievable!

This photo shows a python eating a rat whole! Pythons are so big themselves they can crush big animals and slowly consume them. Pythons have even been known to eat goats.

Did you know?

▲ The Australian **bandy bandy** has a very strict diet – it only eats one type of snake called a blind snake. It can eat a blind snake that is the same size as itself!

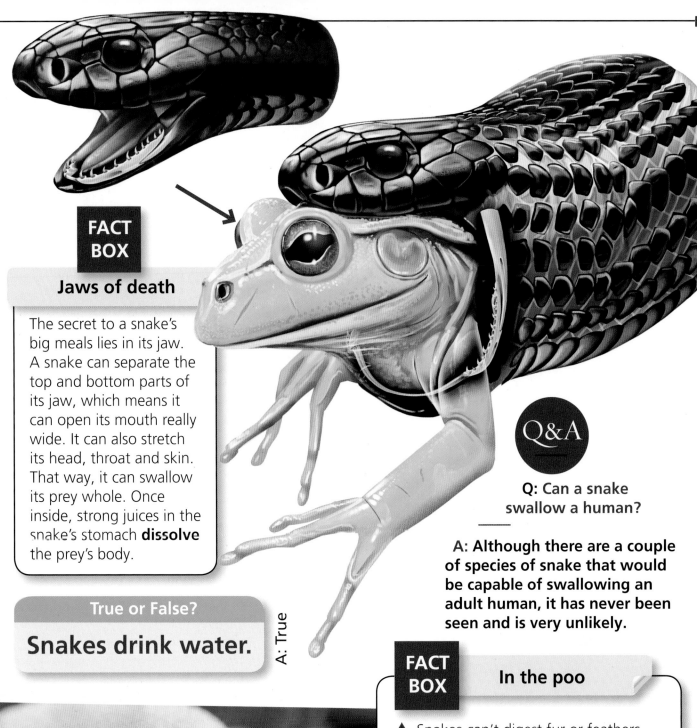

Jaws of death

The secret to a snake's big meals lies in its jaw. A snake can separate the top and bottom parts of its jaw, which means it can open its mouth really wide. It can also stretch its head, throat and skin. That way, it can swallow its prey whole. Once inside, strong juices in the snake's stomach **dissolve** the prey's body.

True or False?

Snakes drink water.

A: True

Q&A

Q: Can a snake swallow a human?

A: Although there are a couple of species of snake that would be capable of swallowing an adult human, it has never been seen and is very unlikely.

FACT BOX

In the poo

▲ Snakes can't digest fur or feathers, beaks or eggshells. This stuff comes out the other end, as snake poo. Snake poo is mushy and messy, and usually dark brown. Sometimes it has a streak of white in it.

A snooze after lunch

After eating, a snake needs its energy to digest, so it becomes **dormant**. The amount of time it takes to finish digesting depends on the size of the snake, the size of its meal, and the temperature of its surroundings. Snakes don't need to eat very often, particularly after a big meal.

WHERE DO SNAKES LIVE?

Snakes live all over the world! Whether it's desert or rainforest, flat or mountainous, grassy or rocky – snakes have figured out a way to survive there. Here we explore the different types of places that snakes live in Australia.

BEAT THE HEAT

Deserts

The desert areas of Australia are very dry and can get very hot during the day. Snakes that live in these places will often shelter under rocks, in cracks in the ground, or in burrows until the temperature drops and they can go out hunting. The woma python is a snake that lives in Australian deserts; it often takes shelter in rabbit burrows during the day and only hunts at night.

Did you know?

The female amethystine python is usually longer and heavier than the male.

Forests

Snakes love forests, as there are plenty of animals to eat and plenty of places to find shelter and protection. Quite a few snakes like to live and hunt in trees – like this amethystine python. Its tail is specially designed to help it grip onto branches and move through trees.

Other good places for snakes in forests are in hollow logs or under fallen tree branches, or under dead leaves lying on the ground. The black-striped snake is one species that takes shelter on the ground. It likes to eat small lizards.

Oceans

There are lots of snakes that spend time in the water. In fact, some snakes don't ever leave the ocean, and give birth to live young underwater, like this olive sea snake.

Mountains ▼

Snakes don't really like the cold, so there are only a few species that live in the mountains in Australia, where the weather is much cooler. The copperhead snake is one species that doesn't mind lower temperatures. Snakes that live in cool places in Australia generally give birth to live young, because eggs would not survive the cold.

Waterways

Snakes are good swimmers, and some snakes spend their whole lives in water. File snakes, like the Arafura file snake, live in rivers and billabongs in northern Australia. They eat fish – catching them by biting them and then gripping on to them with their rough skin.

Grasslands

Grasslands are flat, open places that are mainly covered with grass. They provide shelter for many different animals, including snakes. This collared whip snake likes grasslands, where it feeds mainly on lizards. Other examples of snakes living in grasslands are brown snakes and tiger snakes.

PYTHONS

Green python

The green python spends a lot of its time in trees. When it is ready to hunt, it hangs from a branch by the end of its tail and snatches **prey** with its mouth. Then it brings its prey up to the branch to kill and eat it. A baby green python is actually bright yellow!

The big squeeze

Pythons are constrictors, which means they kill their prey by squeezing them to death. They wrap their big, strong bodies around the body of their prey, and squeeze so tightly that the animal **suffocates.** Then they uncoil themselves and swallow their prey whole.

Fact File ▼

Found: in countries where there is plenty of warm weather and water, including Australia

Live: in caves or trees, also cities and towns

Breeding: egg-laying

Diet: small animals such as lizards, birds, mammals, rodents, and larger animals like pigs, goats, cats and chickens

SNAKE SCALE — PAINFUL BITE

Length: shortest is 60 centimetres; longest 9 metres.

Did you know?

The longest snake species was the African python, which lived millions of years ago. It was longer than a school bus!

Did you know?

A mother python keeps her eggs warm by coiling around them and shivering her muscles.

This beautiful snake is a carpet python. It is found across most of Australia, and it can grow very long – about as long as two grown men lying end to end!

SLITHERIN'

A snake moves by slithering, right? Right.
But did you know there's more than one way to slither?

There are four basic ways a snake moves:

1 **SERPENTINE** This is the most common way snakes move, and probably what you picture when you think of a snake slithering. The snake forms an 'S' shape with its body and pushes against things on the ground such as grass, rocks or twigs, to move forward.

2 **SIDEWINDING** If the snake is travelling across loose or smooth surfaces, such as sand or mud, it will use a motion called sidewinding. It lifts most of its body off the ground and launches itself sideways. It looks a little bit like the snake is jumping sideways across the ground.

3 **CATERPILLAR** This is just what it sounds like – the snake moves the same way as a caterpillar. Instead of its body making curves from side to side, its curves are up and down. This is useful if the snake is in a tight space that doesn't allow it to curve sideways.

4 **CONCERTINA** If a snake wants to climb **vertically**, for example up the trunk of a tree, it uses the concertina movement. First it stretches its head and front of body forward. Then it bunches the middle of its body up and uses its belly scales to get a grip on the tree, and then brings its back end and tail up. By doing this over and over, the snake will slowly climb the tree.

Did you know?

Some snakes don't slither on the ground much at all – they spend most of their time in trees.

FLATTEN AND FLY

FACT BOX

Flying snakes!

It's true – some snakes can fly! A flying snake will launch itself off a tree branch, flatten its body and glide through the air, kind of like a Frisbee. They can't fly upwards, like birds can, but they can travel up to 100 metres – which is as long as a football field! Unfortunately these snakes don't live in Australia – you would have to travel to Southeast Asia, China or India to see a snake fly.

ATTACK AND DEFENCE

Snakes have spent millions of years perfecting their skills for capturing prey and staying alive. Here are some of the ways snakes hunt and protect themselves.

FACT BOX — Hide and strike

Some snakes will lie in wait at a spot where prey is likely to be – for example, under a rock where lizards like to sun themselves, or in a tree that attracts birds or mammals. When the prey comes within reach…WHAM! The snake strikes out and catches its prey by surprise. This method of hunting is called an ambush.

FACT BOX — Can't see me!

Camouflage is a very useful tool for snakes. It helps them hunt and keeps them safe from predators because the colour and pattern on their skin blends in with their background. You can see how this taipan (right) might be hard to spot from a distance. The green tree snake (above) even has white spots that look like sunlight filtering through leaves.

Rough-scaled pythons have long teeth, making their threat display super-effective.

FACT BOX

A trap in the tail

Ever noticed how the tip of a snake's tail looks like a worm? Some snakes, like the southern copperhead, use this to their advantage. They hide and wiggle the end of their tail just like a worm. When a hungry bird or mammal comes in for a taste, it gets a very nasty surprise!

FACT BOX

On the prowl

Some snakes actively hunt for their food. They use their amazing sense of smell to track down animals that might be sleeping in burrows. The whip snake even cruises around until it spots an animal such as a lizard, then chases it!

FACT BOX

Snaky tricks

Some snakes use pretty clever tricks to stay safe. The hognosed snake, from North and South America, pretends to be dead when it senses trouble. Predators prefer live animals, so they leave it alone. Another American trickster, the milk snake, is harmless, but it copies the colours of a venomous coral snake, which scares predators away.

GWARDAR

Did you know?

The gwardar can change colour with the season.

Fact File ▼

Found: across most of Australia

Lives: likes hiding under things like fallen tree branches or rocks, piles of rubbish or building materials, or in burrows and cracks in the ground.

Breeding: lays about 20 eggs at a time

Diet: lizards, birds, mice and other small animals

SNAKE SCALE — DEADLY

Length: up to 1.8 metres

Well hidden

This is one of Australia's most deadly, common and widespread snakes… BUT it rarely bothers humans. (Phew!) It's a type of brown snake, so it is very venomous. It comes in a range of colours and patterns, including orange with a black head, and light brown with thick black stripes.

Sharp eyes

While most snakes rely on their sense of smell to track prey, the gwardar has very good eyesight and will often spot its dinner rather than smell it.

Daytime hunter

The gwardar prefers to hunt during the day, but if the weather is very hot then it will wait until the afternoon or evening to get out and about.

Lightning fast

The gwardar is very quick, which might explain why humans don't often see it. When it strikes, it holds on to its prey and sometimes wraps its body around it, to make absolutely sure it won't lose its dinner!

AUSTRALIA'S MOST VENOMOUS

There are about **100 venomous species** of snake in Australia but not all of them could give you a bite that could kill. Remember: snakes are not naturally **aggressive** – they would much rather stay out of your way than bite you. So don't be afraid!

▼ TAIPAN

The taipan is one of the most feared snakes in Australia. It has the longest fangs, extremely powerful venom, it is aggressive if disturbed and it is incredibly fast moving! It lives in burrows and hollow logs along the coast in Queensland and northern Australia.

▲ MULGA

Also known as the king brown snake, the mulga is mainly brown and lives across most of Australia. It can be very dangerous and aggressive – if it is threatened, it will strike more than once. Luckily for us, it prefers to eat mice, rats, birds and lizards.

Q: What is the difference between poison and venom?

A: Venom is injected, while poison is swallowed or inhaled.

◀ COMMON DEATH ADDER

The death adder has a short, thick body and quite a big head. It spends the day buried in the sand or under leaves or bushes. While other snakes move away when a human approaches, the death adder lies still. This makes it easy to step on.

▼ EASTERN BROWN SNAKE

Just like its name suggests, this is a brown-coloured snake that lives mostly in eastern Australia. It likes to hang around farms and other places where it will find lots of mice. When threatened, it will lift the front part of its body up and flatten its head – which makes it look very nasty!

Did you know?

There is enough venom in one bite from a fierce snake to kill 200,000 mice!

▲ FIERCE SNAKE

This is the most venomous land snake in the world! However, it isn't fierce, as its name suggests. It is actually very **timid**. It lives mostly in very remote areas in Australia and its favourite food is long-haired rats. It grows to about 2 metres long, which is about the same as the height of a door.

▼ TIGER SNAKE

The tiger snake is responsible for many of the snakebites that occur in eastern Australia, mainly because it lives in areas where there are more humans. It is also not as shy as other snakes, so it will let a human get quite close before moving away. When it feels threatened, it flattens its head like a cobra and hisses.

SNAKEBITE SAFETY

As long as you know how to avoid getting bitten by a snake, and what to do in case you are, you can stay safe!

FACT BOX
Why do snakes bite?

The main reason snakes bite is to get food. Venomous snakes will strike and inject venom into their prey to kill or **immobilise** it and make it easier to eat. Non-venomous snakes will bite to grab hold of their prey. The other reason snakes bite is for defence. Snakes are generally not aggressive; they will try to escape first, and will only bite if they feel threatened.

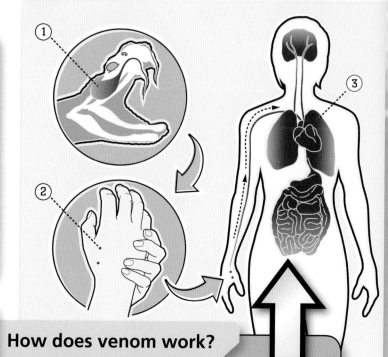

FACT BOX
How does venom work?

▶ Most venomous snakes in Australia have chemicals in their venom called neurotoxins. **1** The neurotoxins enter the blood **2**, where they travel to organs such as the lungs and heart **3** and start to shut them down. This is a very effective way of bringing down an animal that might be much larger or stronger than the snake. Unfortunately, the venom works on humans in the same way. This is why venomous snakes in Australia are so dangerous to humans.

FACT BOX
Magic medicine

Antivenom is a medicine that is injected into someone who has been bitten by a venomous snake. The antivenom stops the body from reacting to the snake's venom. Thankfully, there are antivenoms for most of Australia's dangerous snakes, so as long as you get to a doctor or hospital quickly, you can be treated.

Did you know?

You can be bitten by a **dead snake!** For a few hours after it has died, a snake still has a biting reflex.

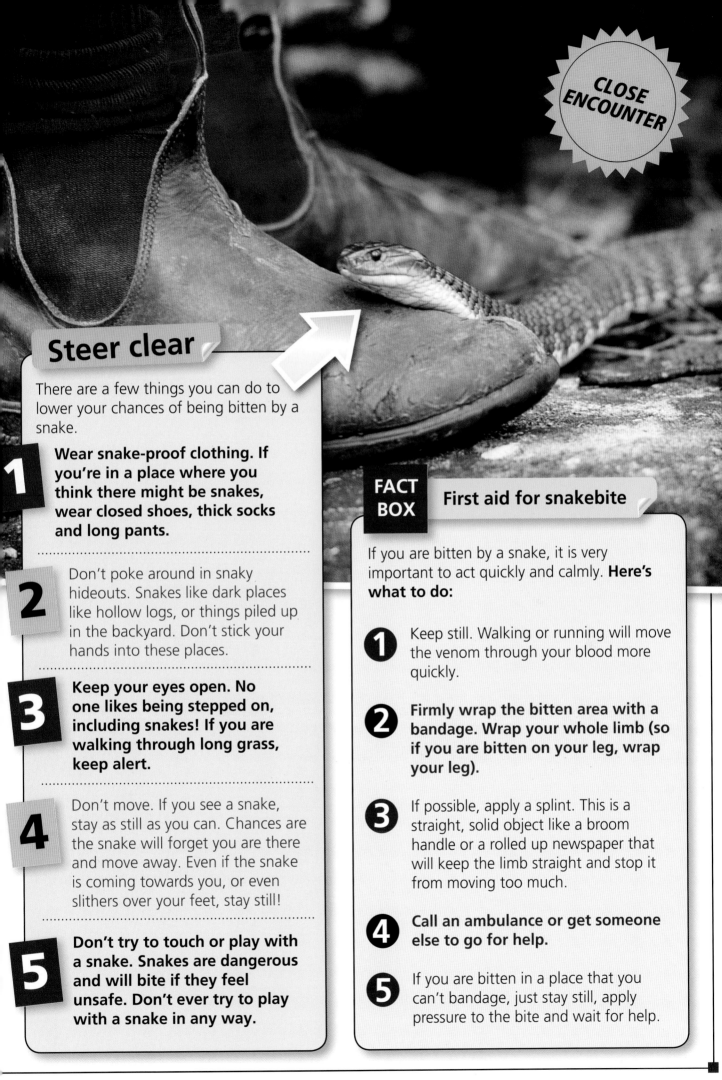

Steer clear

There are a few things you can do to lower your chances of being bitten by a snake.

1 **Wear snake-proof clothing. If you're in a place where you think there might be snakes, wear closed shoes, thick socks and long pants.**

2 Don't poke around in snaky hideouts. Snakes like dark places like hollow logs, or things piled up in the backyard. Don't stick your hands into these places.

3 **Keep your eyes open. No one likes being stepped on, including snakes! If you are walking through long grass, keep alert.**

4 Don't move. If you see a snake, stay as still as you can. Chances are the snake will forget you are there and move away. Even if the snake is coming towards you, or even slithers over your feet, stay still!

5 **Don't try to touch or play with a snake. Snakes are dangerous and will bite if they feel unsafe. Don't ever try to play with a snake in any way.**

FACT BOX — First aid for snakebite

If you are bitten by a snake, it is very important to act quickly and calmly. **Here's what to do:**

1 Keep still. Walking or running will move the venom through your blood more quickly.

2 **Firmly wrap the bitten area with a bandage. Wrap your whole limb (so if you are bitten on your leg, wrap your leg).**

3 If possible, apply a splint. This is a straight, solid object like a broom handle or a rolled up newspaper that will keep the limb straight and stop it from moving too much.

4 **Call an ambulance or get someone else to go for help.**

5 If you are bitten in a place that you can't bandage, just stay still, apply pressure to the bite and wait for help.

SEA-SNAKES

Fact File ▼

Found: mainly in warm tropical waters around the world

Breeding: give birth to live young

Diet: fish, eels, fish eggs

Length: <between about 40cm and 3m:

SNAKE SCALE

VARIES FROM PAINFUL BITE TO FATAL

Turtle-headed sea-snake Eats only fish eggs. ▶

▼ **Leaf-scaled sea-snake**
Small and quite rare, this snake has very small fangs and only a small amount of venom. It eats small fish and likes to spend time on the seabed, rather than close to the surface.

FACT BOX **Serpents of the sea**

Snakes really do live everywhere – even in the ocean! Sea-snakes look a bit like eels, with paddle-like tails to help them swim. Most of them live entirely in the water and can't move on land. Unlike fish, however, they have to come to the surface to breathe. Here are a few sea-snakes found in Australian waters.

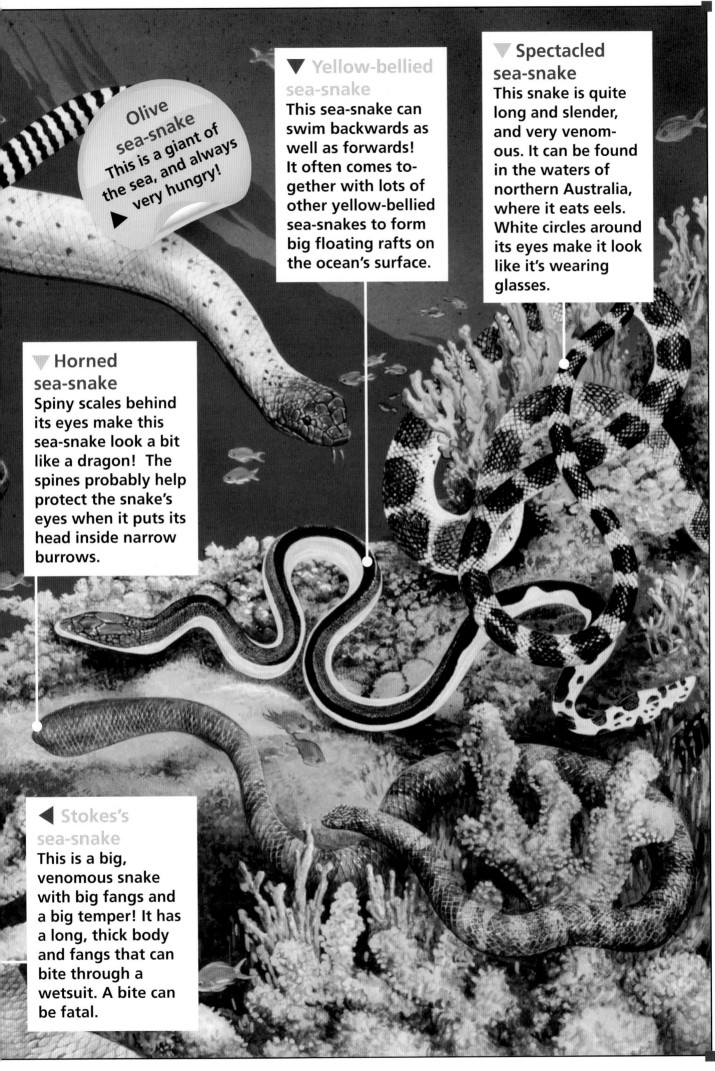

Olive sea-snake
This is a giant of the sea, and always very hungry! ▶

▼ Yellow-bellied sea-snake
This sea-snake can swim backwards as well as forwards! It often comes together with lots of other yellow-bellied sea-snakes to form big floating rafts on the ocean's surface.

▼ Spectacled sea-snake
This snake is quite long and slender, and very venomous. It can be found in the waters of northern Australia, where it eats eels. White circles around its eyes make it look like it's wearing glasses.

▼ Horned sea-snake
Spiny scales behind its eyes make this sea-snake look a bit like a dragon! The spines probably help protect the snake's eyes when it puts its head inside narrow burrows.

◀ Stokes's sea-snake
This is a big, venomous snake with big fangs and a big temper! It has a long, thick body and fangs that can bite through a wetsuit. A bite can be fatal.

WANTED: SNAKES

Lots of people find snakes very useful, including doctors and their patients, scientists and farmers. These people want to use snakes for good reasons. Unfortunately, there are also people who want to use snakes for bad reasons – such as to sell overseas or to turn into products like handbags.

FASHION ITEMS

Did you know?

Snakeskin is also used to make special types of musical in China and Japan.

FACT BOX

Life savers

Doctors and scientists use snake venom to help them make medicine for humans. To do this, they **"milk"** the snake by getting it to bite into a special cup to catch the venom. Snake venom is used to create antivenom, which can save the life of someone who is bitten. Scientists are also using venom to develop medicine for serious sicknesses such as heart disease and cancer.

SNAKES HELP PEOPLE

FACT BOX

Pest controllers

Farmers like snakes because they eat mice, rats, insects and other animals that can destroy their food crops. Snakes can be useful in the garden too – although you might prefer not to have a snake in your vegie patch!

FACT BOX

Sssstealing

Why would anyone steal a snake? The answer is money. Many Australian snakes are smuggled out of the country and sold **illegally** for lots of money. If a person is caught smuggling a snake, he or she will be fined a lot of money and might have to go to jail.

FACT BOX

Yum, yum!

Some Aboriginal people in the Northern Territory hunt file snakes for food. They walk into muddy rivers and feel around with their feet and hands. When they find a file snake, they pull it out of the water and break its neck. Later, they cook the snake over a fire and eat it.

FACT BOX

Pets

Many people like to keep snakes as pets – they are quite easy to look after and only need to be fed every week or two. Some snakes can live in captivity for up to 40 years.

SNAKE BITES

Move around the game board and learn some amazing facts about snakes!

The world's longest snake is the reticulated python, which lives in South-East Asia. It can grow up to 10 metres long and weigh as much as a grown man.

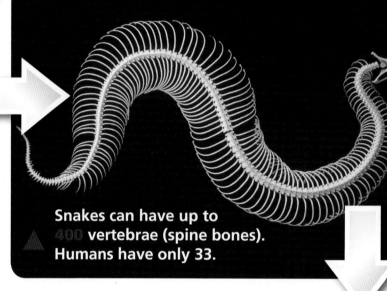

Snakes can have up to 400 vertebrae (spine bones). Humans have only 33.

There IS such thing as a **two-headed snake!** Some snakes are accidentally born with two heads, but they do not survive long.

◀ **All snakes can swim.**

The fastest land snake is the black mamba of Africa. An adult would have trouble outrunning a mamba.

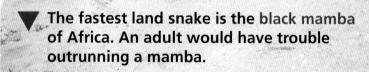

There are no snakes in **Antarctica**, **New Zealand** or **Ireland**.

The spitting cobra of Africa can squirt venom over **2 metres**

A **rattlesnake's tail** is made of hollow, hard shells that rattle when the snake shakes its tail.

Aboriginal people believe many of Australia's rivers and waterholes were made in the Dreamtime by a creation serpent.

Snakes **do not** stop growing, although their growth rate slows down as they get older.

The world's smallest snake is the Barbados threadsnake. It grows to the same length as an iPod, and is about as thin as spaghetti!

Glossary

aggressive	Wanting to attack.
antivenom	A medicine that can stop venom from killing a human.
camouflage	The way an animal or plant disguises itself by looking like it is part of its surroundings.
cold-blooded	An animal whose temperature depends on its surroundings.
consume	Eat.
dissolve	Break down into a liquid.
dormant	Behaving as if asleep.
hibernate	Spend the winter in a safe place being dormant.
illegal	Against the law.
immobilise	To stop something from moving.
immune	Protected from a disease or venom.
particles	Very, very small bits.
predator	An animal that hunts and eats other animals.
prey	An animal that is hunted by other animals.
reflex	An instant reaction.
suffocate	Die from lack of air.
timid	Shy.
vertical	Up and down (instead of side to side).

FURTHER READING

DK Readers: Slinky, scaly snakes
Jennifer Dussling, 2011, DK Publishing

Kids Meet Snakes
Andra Serlin Abramson and
Christopher Mattison, 2013,
Applesauce Press

Time for Kids: Snakes!
2005, Harper Collins

The Australian Geographic web site
www.australiangeographic.com.au